"There are apparently ordinary people who, when they pray, inspire others to open their eyes to see who is there. You can become such a person."

"I am still being blessed by a father and a mother who spoke with God."

Henry B. Eyring, "Families and Prayer," Ensign, September 2015

How to Talk *With* God

Readers' Feedback

"Thank you so much for writing the book, How to Talk *With* God. ... No word or phrase comes to mind that adequately describes my delight and amazement at the results. ... My prayers have become so much more! I am anxious to pray and to see what answers He has for me each day. ... I am simply astounded." —*Tony N.*

"Amazing! ... Gems on every page!

"What you have taught is the most effective tool, in addition to the simplest, I have ever found to come to know Him.

"This book came to me at the perfect time...! I have experienced more fully that The King of the Universe is literally right there, completely available, completely wise, and all-knowing - and speaking to me <u>in volume!</u> Each session brings insights I'd never thought before, increasing my joy and lightening my burdens! ... Such a gift!"
—*Tammy J.*

"The book is incredible. ... I learned that there is truly a predictable and powerful process to talk with God and that He really does want us to talk to Him. ... This book helps everyone know how to communicate with God.... It provides the blueprint for sustained joy...." —*Hugh B.*

"This is a powerful and necessary guide to anyone that wants to find peace and personal revelation in their own lives by really visiting with our most amazing and loving Father." —*Randall V.*

"Wow! ... this is a work long needed by so many! It is powerfully presented from a first person experience perspective, easily understood, and well-articulated. It provides hope to those that have struggled to effectively communicate with deity, and practical, how-to steps for finally getting past the brass ceiling." —*Karl B.*

"This book is absolutely beautiful and so filled with truth. I LOVE how the words of the prophets and the scriptures are interlaced within each principle so that there is more than one witness teaching about what you are saying!

"I LOVE the clear message that God loves me and WANTS to talk with me AND that I CAN talk with Him. I love the metaphors that teach me how simple it is to let go of fears and things that are keeping me back from developing a closer more intimate relationship with Him.

"Learning How to Talk with God in this way has been THE SINGLE MOST IMPORTANT thing I have ever learned to do in my whole life!" —Kellie T.

"I have never even thought that my "journaling" to God could indeed be an opening for a back-and-forth direct communication tool WITH HIM! All this time I have just been "reporting in" and recording my life for posterity.

"The simple outlines are so easy and so....LIBERATING! Why didn't I think of this: Communication is a *conversation* between two people! I am changing my focus, and rather than waiting for a whisper, or a nudging, a prick of the heart, I am EXPECTING daily CONVERSATIONS with Father...!" — *Rene'e L.*

"From the moment I was a few pages in I knew I was reading a God-guided book that is meant to impact the world, substantially. Thank you! The book is amazing." —*Ian S.*

"'How to Talk *With* God' teaches what I want my children to learn the most. The reason I want them to pray, go to church, study the word of God, be good, etc. is so they will have a strong relationship with God. This book teaches them clearly how to do that!" —*Sarah J.*

"I read the whole book yesterday. Wow! It was totally an answer to prayer and helped remind me of who I really am and how to be the person I am meant to be. Thank you so much!" —*Emily W.*

"I have had such a deep longing to hear His voice so that I am doing His will and not mine. I just haven't known how to get from where I have been to there. These writings have given me much hope that I can overcome false thoughts and truly speak with our Father in Heaven and receive answers." —*Janeal S.*

"*How to Talk With God* is what I like to call a 'Rock Solid' book. It is a book that is simple and powerful and allowed me to apply principles immediately. The focus was truly on the Savior and God who are the solid foundation to success. I didn't have to go through any complicated processes or try to learn something new or difficult. *How to Talk With God* helped me gain a deeper relationship with God and realize that to talk with God is much easier than I usually make it out to be." —*Tyler W.*

How to Talk *With* God

*A simple guide for anyone who wants to begin
or improve their communication with God*

William S. Black

foreword

Kellie Rae Turley

Acknowledgements

I DEDICATE THIS BOOK to my Father in Heaven who gave me the assignment to write it and then provided the way and the means to do it.

I express my gratitude and love to Audrey for saying "yes" 26 years ago and then never changing her mind. She is the most amazing woman I have ever known. Her faith in God and her support to me through thick and mostly thin is beyond extraordinary.

To my six beautiful children: Thank you for loving me in spite of my many quirks and mistakes. Thank you for listening. Thank you for putting God first in your lives and never giving up.

To my parents, Audrey's parents, and all our brothers and sisters: Thank you for your help, prayers, love, and support over *all* years.

To my friends and mentors Roger Anthony (1942-2014), Clay Stevens, and Kellie Rae Turley: Thank you for believing in me, teaching me, learning with me, standing by me and changing my life.

Thank you Audrey, Kellie, Tammy Jensen, Karl Black, Brent Davis, and Rene'e La Montagne for reading, commenting, and proofing the first drafts; thank you Maria "Ren" Black (and your able assistant and husband Stanley) for reading, commenting, editing and teaching me as you went along. Your insights and feedback were invaluable to this work.

Table of Contents

Foreword i

Introduction iii

PART 1: BEGIN 1

Who do you want to talk with?................................ 1

Desire it!... 3

Become familiar with His voice 5

Talk to Him like a normal person 6

Write your prayers to Him and record His responses .. 7

Ask Him questions..................................... 8

Don't be afraid to talk with God................... 10

Keep it simple.. 12

PART 2: IMPROVE 17

Be patient with yourself............................. 17

Be grateful.. 20

Choose to believe...................................... 22

Fear not 23

Turn off the noise of the world 25

Avoid doubts and second guessing 30

One-word answers or feelings or pictures are ok 34

PART 3: CONTINUE 43

    Keep wanting it! 43

    Persist! 46

    Be obedient! 50

    Harness the power of forgiveness 51

SUMMARY 57

APPENDIX 60

    Ask, and ye shall receive 60

    Examples of personal revelations 66

    Some final thoughts 81

Foreword

My Dear Brothers and Sisters:

Since my childhood I have always had a close relationship with God. I have always known of His presence and His desire to talk with me.

My conversations with God began as I walked through desert washes and mountain tops of my native Arizona. After these talks, I would go home and write what was spoken. These conversations turned into a written dialogue between God and me, which deepened our relationship even more.

My desire is that the people I love—*all of you*—have a similar experience with God and prayer. You don't have to wait days, weeks, months, or years to hear God's voice. You can receive the answers, the direction, and the peace you seek right now. And even more important, I hope each one of you comes to know of your great worth in God's eyes and heart. I want each of you to know that you are literally a child of God who loves you, wants to spend time with you, and has words He wants to speak to you.

I prayed to be able to reach more people, so that I could share my message of the deep beauty and richness that can come from having personal conversations with God. My prayers were answered and God sent William Black into my life.

After many months of talking with him and sharing my own conversations with God, William has taken it upon himself to develop his own *closer* relationship with God. And now William shares with everyone in "How to Talk With God," a simple, beautiful way to bridge the gap we often feel in trying to hear and feel God's word, will and love for us.

It is no mistake God brought William and me together, and now God brings *all of us* together through the words of this book.

If you have the slightest desire to create a relationship with God, or improve your relationship and communication with Him, I give you the same invitation I gave William, the same invitation God gives to all of us to learn of Him, to spend time with Him, to talk with Him, to come unto Him. I invite you to read this book and practice what is taught here and see for yourself...God wants to speak *with* you!

May you be blessed and may you prosper in the ways of the Lord, for God desires to talk with you!

With a heart full of love and gratitude,

Kellie Rae Turley

Introduction

You'd think that over 40 years of believing and being active in my church would be enough to teach me everything I'd want to know about communicating with God. I've had too many spiritual experiences to even begin to count. But like the plaque on the wall of my high school English classroom declared, "It's what you learn after you think you know it all that really counts."

This deeper learning came when a series of major trials hit our family in rapid succession beginning in 2006. Any of these by themselves was more than enough. All of them together, one after another, were simply too much to handle; I couldn't do it. Business reversals, lawsuits, prolonged financial crisis, family trauma, and my baby daughter's brain tumor and cancer fight wiped me out.

I shudder to think how close I came to losing everything that matters most. What we went through was so hard emotionally, spiritually, financially and physically that at points I felt myself going numb from pain and witnessed what the jaws of hell must be. Only by God's pure grace am I still alive, married with family intact. Because of His most tender mercies I am filled with faith and hope.

God rescued me and pulled me out of dark places again and again while bringing healing and help of *every* kind. Consequently, my love for Him is intense and my gratitude overflowing. I owe *everything* to Him and cannot repay even the smallest part. In one of these darkest, most painful times I learned for myself that God is as close as you allow Him to be. He has real power that I'd read about a thousand times but then experienced firsthand. This was when I gained a sure knowledge that God hears and does answer our sincere prayers. I learned that answers could come in real-time. I also discovered that you can figure out almost anything just from asking God "Yes / No" questions and getting really good at detecting what each of those two responses feels like to you personally. Once you have that difference clear then you can have confidence receiving and acting upon this most basic form of personal revelation.

When you really, *really* need to know and are willing to ask with great intensity or desire of your whole soul, God will reveal His arm of mercy to you in a way you can understand. Already, He is helping to lift and bless you anonymously behind the scenes. Trust this even if in the beginning it doesn't make sense or you can't comprehend it. It's real. When the scripture says He stands at the door and knocks and wants us to open the door for Him, that's as literal as anything I've ever come to know. He's right there. Right there!

During the toughest times when I desperately needed relief and help I would go to the most sacred place I could find where I believed I would literally be closer to God. Here I could be separate from the noise of the world and quiet the noise in my mind. Over time, I learned that other places could be quiet, reverent places for me in moments when I really needed heavenly help and inspiration. Places in my home, my office at work, a park—I found other good spots where the Spirit could touch my soul especially during early morning hours.

In 2013 I met Kellie Rae Turley who for decades has been writing her prayers in notebooks *as she prays.* She was part of an organization my company was mentoring. At some point she opened up about the way she prays and the revelation that's a natural part of this flowing communication with God. To say I was fascinated is truly an understatement. Here was a normal person doing exactly what the scriptures suggest—asking and receiving.

For months I pushed her to tell me more. She patiently explained things that amazed me not so much because of their complexity or mystery but because of their simplicity. How could I have missed it? Such simple principles hidden in plain sight that resonated with everything I believe! Even with her encouragement and my growing desire to experience this for myself, it still took me nearly half a year to make the kind of effort on a regular basis that yielded results similar to what Kellie had been sharing. To pray in such a conversational way took significantly more effort than the passive way of daily praying with which I was more familiar. It definitely took some getting used to.

This book came as a direct result of learning how to talk with God in this more abundant way. I will be forever grateful Kellie was willing to share and can never thank her enough.

I claim no special powers, gifts, abilities, or privileges to communicate with God. I have only that which is available to all of God's children. I did, however, ask earnestly for help with it and have been willing to keep at it. Because I have been so blessed I have desired to share—with any who will listen—the knowledge I have of the great goodness of God and His amazing love.

However, it was not my idea to create this little book. As I prayed on Saturday, May 9, 2015 I was given clear instruction to record my experience in learning how to communicate more effectively with God. I was promised that through this assignment would come "greater clarity" and answers to prayers "concerning [my] children that they might connect directly with [God] and not be dependent on [me] but only on [Him]."

What you're about to read are simple truths I've learned firsthand that are as precious to me as oxygen. Indeed, in many instances, the lessons that made this understanding possible quite literally took my breath away.

I take full responsibility for the contents, though I've listed a number of resources throughout that indicate I'm far from being the only one learning and applying these truths. Indeed, as mentioned above I wouldn't have even written these few pages had I not been told in a very personal way to share what I'd learned in laymen's terms so everyone that wants to can understand.

I invite you to receive this as the precious gift it is, with all the love and encouragement I know God has for you and is sending to you even at this very moment!

"If thou shalt ask,

thou shalt receive revelation upon revelation,

knowledge upon knowledge,

that thou mayest know

the mysteries and peaceable things—

that which bringeth joy,

that which bringeth life eternal."

D&C 42:61

"We are strengthened by the truth that the greatest force in the world today is the power of God as it works through man. To sail safely the seas of mortality, we need the guidance of that Eternal Mariner—even the great Jehovah. We reach out, we reach up to obtain heavenly help. ... Our Heavenly Father will not leave our sincere petition unanswered."

Thomas S. Monson, "Guided Safely Home," *Ensign*, November 2014

"If you want to stay close to someone who has been dear to you, but from whom you are separated, you know how to do it. You would find a way to speak to them, you would listen to them, and you would discover ways to do things for each other. The more often that happened, the longer it went on, the deeper would be the bond of affection. If much time passed without the speaking, the listening, and the doing, the bond would weaken.

"God is perfect and omnipotent, and you and I are mortal. But He is our Father, He loves us, and He offers the same opportunity to draw closer to Him as would a loving friend. And you will do it in much the same way: speaking, listening, and doing."

Henry B. Eyring, Facebook, July 28, 2015

"No Father would send His children off to a distant, dangerous land for a lifetime of testing where Lucifer was known to roam free without first providing them with … means to communicate with Him from Father to child and from child to Father. …We are, none of us, left here alone without hope of guidance…"

Boyd K. Packer, "Prayer and Promptings," Ensign, November 2009

Begin
Decide you want to talk with Him
Desire it!
Become familiar with God's voice
Talk to Him like a normal person
Write your prayers to Him and record His responses
Ask Him questions
Don't be afraid to talk with Him
Keep it simple

PART 1: BEGIN

God lives and He's interested in you! You can have a personal relationship with Him. In fact, He wants to talk to you. He longs to be a part of your life.

Whether this is old news or new news, if you want to improve your communication with God, *openness is the key*.

This is the roadmap I was given by trial and error—and lots of help from angel mentors. I'm not hoping it's true or that it works. *I know it's true and that it works!* In fact, what took me *years* to figure out, can be yours in much less time—even days—*if* you want it.

Please don't let anything keep you from this journey. I'll take you step by step through the process.

Let's begin!

Who do you want to talk with?

Let's face it, we listen to who we want to listen to and talk to the people we're interested in talking to. Each of us is listening all the time—to someone—and we have conversations all the time. None of this is new. There are people we listen to and talk to every day. On the other hand there's a whole bunch of people we never talk to because: (1) we don't know them, (2) we have no reason to, (3) we don't know how to contact them, or (4) they aren't talking to us.

The same is true about God. We won't talk to Him if we: (1) don't know Him, (2) have no reason to talk to Him, (3) don't know how to contact Him, or (4) don't realize He is talking to us all the time.

It's not that people don't know how to hear or even receive personal revelation; it's more that they don't know how to stop the kind of personal revelation that's hurting them and tune into the kind that helps.

Not every discussion, not every voice we listen to makes us happy. The father of lies has been barging in for so long we're numb to his abuse. Do you really think that voice in your head that speaks of everything that's wrong with you and invites you to worry, fear, and doubt about everything is your own voice? Not a chance! Your mind has been hacked and filled with stuff that just isn't true but unfortunately has become very familiar. This is an example of harmful personal revelation: (1) it doesn't come from God, and (2) its purpose is to hurt or weigh you down.

> "And behold, others he flattereth away, and telleth them there is no hell; and he saith unto them: I am no devil, for there is none—and thus he whispereth in their ears, until he grasps them with his awful chains, from whence there is no deliverance."
> 2 Nephi 28:22

Never before in the history of the world have there been so many messages and voices banging all at the same time. It's super noisy and almost never quiet anymore.

Here's where trials and challenges can be truly

helpful. The world is like a big auditorium where everyone is talking before the show. You can hear the buzz of a thousand conversations all around you. Trials are like the announcer that enters and gets everyone to focus, stop talking, turn off their cell phones, and pay attention to the performance that's on the stage. We might miss the point of the whole "show" of life if we were so distracted that we didn't quiet down, watch, and listen. Thus, trials can be beneficial in inviting us to turn to God and engage with Him.

When your desire to know Him and your need for Him becomes the most important thing in your life, communication with Him is straightforward. You can shift away from the negative and begin enjoying personal revelation from Him that lifts, inspires and fills you with courage and faith.

> "How can this gift be ours? It comes through a matter of personal revelation. … In this process, seeking for personal revelation is a key. … As you seek a personal witness—your personal revelation—you will discover that Heavenly Father has provided a special way for you to know the truth for yourself…" Robert D. Hales, "Eternal Life—to Know Our Heavenly Father and His Son, Jesus Christ," *Ensign*, Nov. 2014

Desire it!

We've all received exactly the same amount from God: exactly not enough! God wants to communicate with us in a personal, interactive way. When it comes to our time, He wants more than our leftovers. Think how difficult it is to carry on a conversation with someone who is disinterested. Talking *with* God begins with the desire to have a meaningful interaction with Him.

As a boy my family would visit my grandma and grandpa. On arrival, I'd dutifully pause a few short moments for the necessary pleasantries, but inside, I was chomping at the bit to run out back and play ball with the cousins. I loved my grandma and grandpa but they just weren't as interesting to me as the things I wanted to do. It never made sense to me why the adults sat around and just never stopped talking.

As I grew, I became curious about my grandparents and their lives. Unfortunately, by then, I didn't have much time left with them. Contrary to my childhood beliefs, they weren't boring at all. They had so much wisdom and knowledge, plus they had all these stories to share. Not once did they drag me into their house, sit me down, and make me listen to all they had to say.

I think our view of God can be like how I viewed my grandparents: un-relatable, not approachable, kind of boring, less exciting than my worldly interests, and distant. Nothing could be further from the truth. God is amazing! He's wonderful, powerful, interesting, loving, completely approachable, and close—really close. No matter how incredible He is or how much He has to offer, He won't force you to get to know Him or receive anything you don't want to receive.

Whether you're rich or poor, educated or not, old or young, spiritual or not—God wants to talk with you. Most everyone is stuck in the ruts of a world pretending everything somehow spontaneously appeared or evolved over billions of years. Even believers get stuck in limiting ruts—sometimes deeper ruts because they think they're already so enlightened they don't need much more from God.

If your relationship with God is vague, undefined, non-existent, boring, un-fulfilling, or lackluster in anyway, then start by desiring something better. If you feel there's something more or something you're missing out on, you're right! So many people are actually experiencing forms of homesickness and don't know it. We were with our Father in Heaven before we came to earth and we miss Him! If we've forgotten Him or don't know how to really talk with Him, the fact remains: we are all His children. He loves us and we love Him, even if our temporary, spiritual amnesia has blocked the memory.

Become familiar with His voice

Anybody who wants to converse with God and have a regular, normal relationship with Him must become familiar with His voice. This is not difficult. It's just different from what we're used to. It starts with reading the words God has revealed to prophets dating clear back to Adam. It continues with hearing the words God reveals to prophets in our modern day. When you read or listen to scriptures, you become familiar with His voice. Familiarity comes from regularity and consistency over time. Reading the scriptures every day is vital.

Your confidence grows as you come to realize that God is consistent. When the personal instructions and insights you receive from Him match up with His words found in the scriptures and spoken by modern prophets, you don't have to wonder if it's really from Him. Soon you discover that many of the personal revelations you receive will help you understand His Word more fully. He helps you discern where un-helpful philosophies of man have crept in to change or water down His doctrine.

Talk to Him like a normal person

How would you like it if someone came to you speaking in a monotone voice saying the same thing over and over? Or how would you feel if someone treated you like an animal at the zoo that we briefly gawk at or even squawk at and then all-too-quickly move on? God is not an attendant at the drive up window of your local fast food restaurant. If your attitudes with Him are shallow, your relationship with Him will be shallow and polite—at best.

Instead, think of a counselor or trusted friend. How do you converse with them? Not everyone can relate to what it's like to have a kind and loving parent. Divorce, death and abuse impact all of us directly or indirectly. This can cause hesitation or doubt when it comes to accepting the notion of a divine, even familial connection with a perfect being. Yet accepting this is exactly what I'm encouraging you to do.

God loves you as a Heavenly Father. Just like an earthly friend or loved one, God cares about what you're doing at school, at work, at home—everything in your life.

Communication with Him about what's important to you can be as real and normal as picking up the phone and calling home.

Write your prayers to Him and record His responses

Nothing you do to figure out your relationship with God will change your communication with Him faster than writing to Him and recording His responses. Kneel or sit

> "For I command all … that they shall write the words which I speak unto them…" 2 Nephi 29:11

with a notebook or computer—whatever is most comfortable for you. The important thing here is that you shift away from your natural tendencies that can be sloppy or passive. Write to Him about what's really on your mind. Not only will it set you up to get answers and feedback from Him, you'll also become much clearer about your concerns. There will be less noise rattling around in your head when it's out and written down.

This takes effort and those efforts are worth it! This can feel awkward at first, maybe even a little irreverent. Yet when answers come—and they will—you'll find it helpful that you are in a position to record His words to

> "Inspiration carefully recorded shows God that His communications are sacred to us. Recording will also enhance our ability to recall revelation." Richard G. Scott, "How to Obtain Revelation and Inspiration for Your Personal Life," *Ensign*, May 2012

you. There's no "right way" to do this, just like there's no prescribed way to communicate with someone.

Sometimes there's so much on your heart and mind it can feel overwhelming to write it all out. This exercise is not intended to add stress to your life. Do what feels right to you. He wants to talk with you and hopes this will be a two-way street. I'm grateful for the blessing of being able to go back and read the insights, counsel, and instruction. Not everything has been recorded and that's ok.

Keep praying as often as you can whether you record some, all, or none. Experiment with this as you are able and see if things begin to improve in how you approach Him and receive answers from Him. I'm confident this can and will make a difference in your relationship with Him.

Ask Him questions

Years ago, a religion professor taught me that questions are like fish hooks. Just like a fish won't usually jump out of the water into your hands without a hook to hold onto, answers need questions to "hook them" in order to be caught. Keep it simple. I started with yes/no questions— ones that could be answered by a positive or negative feeling. If the answer was yes, it was positive either by a "yes" in my mind or a good feeling like when you get goose bumps. If the answer was "no," it was usually signaled by a lack of positive feelings or thoughts, not necessarily a bad

> "One of the great lessons that each of us needs to learn is to ask. Why does the Lord want us to pray to Him and to ask? Because that is how revelation is received." Richard G. Scott, "How to Obtain Revelation and Inspiration for Your Personal Life," *Ensign*, May 2012

sensation. For some reason I trusted the "no's" more than the "yes's." If a yes came, I would confirm it by asking, "did You just tell me 'yes'?" and the positive signal would happen again. So I learned to gain confidence with the "yes's".

You can ask whatever questions you want; just start asking questions that you really want answers to. After getting more confident with yes/no questions, I started asking questions that required at least a "phrase" response if not a full sentence. Perhaps what surprised me the most was that God often started His answers with something encouraging like, "I love you, William," or "It is well." He knows you way better than you know yourself and loves you intensely. I never grow tired of hearing Him tell me He loves me and this expression of love is never copied by Satan. That's one of the ways I have learned to discern a revelation from God vs. one from the devil. God inspires courage, confidence, and hope. Satan likes to discourage, accuse, and cause worry, fear, or doubt.

Be patient with yourself. Second guessing really messes with your mind. Avoid it! When you feel a "yes," confirm it and trust it. When you hear or feel a short phrase or sentence response, write it down and let it be. Of course you can follow-up with a yes/no question like, "did You just tell me _____?" God doesn't get anxious about stuff but He certainly wants to talk to you. So take heart! Don't be lazy about it but don't over think it either. Satan never wants you to get revelation from any other source but him. And because we are *way* more familiar with worldly revelation than Godly revelation, the devil uses those familiar voices to get us to worry about mistakes. He whispers that we're not getting it right, that we're not worthy, or any number of ridiculous excuses to stop us in our tracks and keep us from walking through this amazing portal of communication with God.

Don't be afraid to talk with God

I have to confess I hate scary movies and people hiding behind corners and jumping out to scare me. (Of course my children and wife find it hugely amusing to do just that!) I can't comprehend why anyone would purposely pay money to watch a horror movie. It just doesn't process in my brain. Whenever there's a story of angels suddenly appearing to people—like on the night of Christ's birth when the angel came to the shepherds at night—the first words of the heavenly messenger are almost always, "fear not." (Can I just say right now that I don't want *any* person or messenger suddenly popping up around me! I've been very clear in my prayers that if God wants to or needs to send an angel to me...please, please, *please* start making some noise long before you get to my room and please start the "fear not" part of your message with lots of repetition well in advance. Just sayin'.)

I mention this only because I know what it's like to think that conversation with God while in our mortal state is reserved for a select few who are called as prophets to relay the words of God to us. It's one thing to take responsibility for what God tells us *through* His ancient and modern

> "Look unto me in every thought; doubt not, fear not."
> D&C 6:36

10

prophets. It can be an entirely different experience when the communication turns really personal. When I realized that God was both willing and eager to speak with me in such a personal way, yes I was excited, but I was also nervous. After all, I wasn't sure what He would say and I kind of like being in control.

If prayer is a one way street, I can kneel down, say what I want to say and be done with it. When prayer becomes a two-way communication, God is now free to tell me whatever He wants to and I'm "obligated" to Him in a different way; I'm accountable now, not just at some future judgment-bar date.

Not surprisingly, I learned that my nervousness to talk to God was influenced by that same being who has been tripping me up my whole life. Passive praying is one thing, active praying with back and forth communication in real-time is not ok if you're trying to herd someone down the path to hell. God speaks the truth and wants us to know how things really are. He exposes how the father of lies actually operates. We can discover how knowing God and Jesus Christ in a very personal way can be the foundation for life now, not just for eternal life in the world to come (see John 17:3).

The more you talk with God the more you learn to trust Him and the more you experience His unrelenting help and support. He never runs you into the ditch. He pulls you out of the ditches and gives you suggestions for how to make your day better. He is willing to be as involved in our life as we want Him to be and every part of our life He touches is better...a lot better. If you want specifics, He helps you with specifics. If you want to keep things more general that's ok, too. He meets you where you are and where you want to be. He will take it at the pace you want to go while always encouraging you to be the best you can and to raise your sights to higher heights. We've been sedated by the world and are largely ignorant of all God wants to give us if we'll only ask. In other words, we settle for far less than what He's willing to give us.

Perhaps the most common invitation (and the most ignored) in all of scriptures is, "Ask, and ye shall receive." Whatever we really want, God is willing to work with us to get it. And because we don't always want what's best for us, God would like to guide us to what's best for us. Whether temporal or spiritual, there is nothing God cannot do or provide. (see Appendix: Examples of personal revelations that have encouraged me—December 17, 2014)

Be confident! God has your best interests in mind. Don't let Satan tell you what God will or won't do for you or how it will or won't make you feel. Go to God directly. I promise you'll be glad you did!

Keep it simple

I like to over think and complicate things. When I was young, I learned an alternative version of the familiar nursery rhyme, *Three Blind Mice*.

Familiar version:

Three blind mice. Three blind mice.
See how they run. See how they run.
They all ran after the farmer's wife,

Who cut off their tails with a carving knife,
Did you ever see such a sight in your life,
As three blind mice?

The new version I learned was fancier and more sophisticated. I loved showing off by singing:

A trio of sightless rodents. A trio of sightless rodents.
Observe how they perambulate. Observe how they perambulate.
They all perambulated after the agriculturalist's spouse,
Who severed their anal extensions with a carving instrument,
Have you ever observed such a spectacle in your existence,
As a trio of sightless rodents?

The older I get, the less impressed I am with "trios of sightless rodents" and the more I crave the simple and unassuming. God is perfect with no insecurities whatsoever. He has no other object but our eternal welfare. In speaking with us, He meets us where we are and speaks our language so that we can really get it.

We're not perfect and we're insecure, so it's easy to fall for the temptation to pretend we're something we're not. We habitually do this around others which can influence the way we talk to God. He's so patient with us. He wants us to relax and be ourselves around Him. He wants our time with Him to be rewarding and enjoyable, not something stressful to be avoided.

Be yourself. That's the only thing you can do better than anyone else!

"Satan perpetrates a terrible lie that his way is easy and My way is hard. The only thing easy about Satan's path of destruction is the ease with which My children fall for it. … Satan appeals to the appetites of the natural man to drag men down. It's literally like giving candy to a baby.

"How does man have a chance, you ask? He doesn't without Me."

Personal Revelation received by Author on June 15, 2015

"Come unto me, all *ye* that labour and are heavy laden, and I will give you rest.

"Take my yoke upon you, and learn of me; for I am meek and lowly in heart: and ye shall find rest unto your souls.

"For my yoke *is* easy, and my burden is light."

Matthew 11:28-30

Improve
Be patient with yourself
Be grateful
Choose to believe
Fear not
Turn off the noise of the world
Avoid doubts and second guessing
One-word answers or feelings or pictures are ok

PART 2: IMPROVE

Be patient with yourself

Since birth we are bombarded with voices and thoughts that erode our sense of self-worth, bind us in fear and leave us hopeless. Soon the negativity becomes so familiar that we say, "That's just life," or "That's just the way I am." That which is familiar over a long time tends to become our comfort zone. The forces of evil have fabricated descriptions of God that simply aren't true. Images of a disinterested entity or one vengefully poised to punish us for every misstep are confusing. Thus we often have a misguided perception of our relationship with God and how He sees us. Many struggle with even a basic construct of what a Father in Heaven could be.

> "It's not that people don't know how to hear or even receive personal revelation; it's more that they don't know how to stop the kind of personal revelation that's hurting them and tune into the kind that helps." From page 2.

In The Family: A Proclamation to the World we learn that "By divine design, fathers are to preside over their families in love and righteousness and are responsible to provide the necessities of life and protection for their families." Any who struggle with a picture of "Father" may start here. He loves us! He is full of light because He is full of righteousness. This simply means He is not distracted by habits or weaknesses that often cause parents to neglect, abuse, or even forsake their children. Our Father in Heaven is right there in all our comings, goings and stayings. He is the ideal for He never tires and is available to talk to, walk with, dream with, and study with 24/7.

He provides all that is necessary for our time here on Earth. He provides and protects to the maximum extent possible within the bounds of our own personal agency— His greatest gift so far.

He is secure and confident in all things so He never bullies or demeans. He always encourages and lifts. Sometimes His messages can feel stern when He warns us of danger. He teaches us to follow His perfect rules or commandments which protect and build us.

When we speak negatively towards ourselves or others, we are practicing and repeating lines from the devil's script book. Constant revelations of darkness are intended to keep us from seeing the truth. They keep us from renewing our relationship with God that began long before we came to Earth. God's scriptures (and personal revelations) never speak with a voice to discourage or breed negativity.

If you desire to follow God and hear His voice, please be willing to believe Him. You will find He always provides a way to overcome every fall or misstep. He loves you and is pleased with any and every effort no matter what the devilish voice may say to the contrary. Keep this in mind as you work to communicate with Father. Give Him every benefit by way of holding Him in the highest regard for that is exactly how He is approaching you. Whatever your past experience with imperfect people, elevate your perception of God to that of a perfect being full of love. You are everything to Him and your success—your eternal success—is paramount to Him.

As difficult as it may be at first, please be patient with yourself. See yourself at your best—like Father does—and this will open more quickly the pathway of communication with God. The evil one masquerades as a gatekeeper to heaven, pretending to know all things, including the rules for engagement with God. Give the devil no heed for he is a liar. He knows nothing of God for he rejected the plan of happiness and seeks only your destruction. Therefore, he has no credentials and standing with God. The main power Satan has is the rut of familiarity. Stop giving him power and influence in your life. The abuse has gone on long enough. You

"Seek the Revelations of the Spirit. If we are not seeking to use this channel of revelation, we are living beneath our ... privileges. ... Revelation... [does] not always come with overwhelming force. ... We start out with a small amount of light—even if it is only a desire to believe. Gradually, ... 'that light groweth brighter and brighter'.... Think of what a glorious thing it is to reach beyond our earthly limitations, to have the eyes of our understanding opened and receive light and knowledge from celestial sources! It is our privilege and opportunity ... to seek personal revelation... " Dieter F. Uchtdorf, "Your Potential, Your Privilege," *Ensign*, May 2011 are a Child of God and as such have privileges beyond your wildest dreams. The possibilities of greatness and goodness are truly without limit. Your interactions and communications with God will unfold these opportunities to your view. As you become more aware, choose to never go back or retreat from this expanding knowledge of who you really are and your relationship with God!

Be grateful

Few things invite the spirit of revelation faster than gratitude. There is a power so real in gratitude it is almost tangible.

Have you ever been around someone who complains? Do you complain? To complain is to blame circumstances and see only what is lacking. Complaining blinds the mind, blocks the Spirit, and drains away power. In the scriptures the word often used instead of complaining is murmuring. The habit of complaining is devastating in that it turns a critical eye toward God as if He is the enemy and it's somehow His fault. Satan uses this tendency to get us to stand with him in opposition to God. Then he feeds us a constant diet of

> "Wherefore because that Satan rebelled against me, and sought to destroy the agency of man … I caused that he should be cast down;
>
> "And he became Satan, yea, even the devil, the father of all lies, to deceive and to blind men, and to lead them captive at his will, even as many as would not hearken unto my voice." Moses 4:3-4

negative emotions to give us more evidence that life is unfair, unjust, and that we've been wronged and can't succeed because of things beyond our control.

Complaining is the gateway for receiving personal revelation from Satan.

Gratitude is the gateway for receiving personal revelation from God.

You can't complain and be grateful at the same time. You can't be grateful and complain at the same time. Choose one or the other but you cannot have both together. If you're getting lots of revelation but it's not the good kind you're looking for, replace criticism, complaining, and negativity with gratitude. That alone will turn the tide toward the good revelation you want—from God.

Looking for the good and thanking God for it is like seeing a few stars in the night sky and then viewing the same night sky through a powerful telescope. What started as few becomes so many we can't possibly count them all. The more we count the more we are drawn to see more.

The power of gratitude starts with recognizing something in our life that is good and then another and another— even if it is really hard at first. Find three things a day you are grateful for and write them down. Do this consistently and you will never, ever come to the end of gratitude for it has no limits. The evidence of good in your life will grow to crowd out the negative. Soon your focus will be on the positive where it is much easier to discern the voice of God.

Choose to believe

There is no such thing as an absence of belief. We believe...in something. And whatever that something is, we gather evidence to support that belief—either consciously or unconsciously. Understanding that belief is a choice awakens new considerations. We have power like a gatekeeper to choose who can enter and who must not.

I received a very personal understanding of this one day as I asked the Lord a lot of questions. I call it the courtroom analogy. This helped me understand why there's such a pull from both "the good side" and also "the bad side." (see APPENDIX: Examples of personal revelations that have encouraged me: Friday, July 11, 2014)

We are the judge in our own courtroom of agency. The lawyers of both sides lay before us their case and we can listen for as long as we choose. The judge holds the right to make a decision or ruling, but also decides how much time to allow for presentation of evidence and entertaining any motions.

This metaphor helped me realize that I don't have to let this proceeding go on and on. I can make decisions and be done with it. In other words, I can choose to believe whichever side I want, make my final ruling and be done with the case. When a "lawyer" from the losing side tries to file another motion after the case is closed, I can simply refer them to the decision that was already made; no need to re-open the case. This has saved me enormous amounts of time and frustration. Indecision is a stressful waste of time that feeds doubt.

Satan doesn't want us to enjoy the peace of deciding in favor of God. He wants to keep us jumping back and forth trying to be "fair" to both sides as if to ensure we are not being blinded or misled.

Stop being fair! The two sides are diametrically opposed to each other! You can't be "fair" to both or you'll be torn to bits in the middle.

One of the best examples I've ever read that completely illustrates this point is found in the Old Testament:

"...choose you this day whom ye will serve; whether the gods which your fathers served that were on the other side of the flood, or the gods of the Amorites, in whose land ye dwell: but as for me and my house, we will serve the Lord." (Joshua 24:15)

The more you choose to believe in God and follow His ways, the easier it is to communicate with Him.

Fear Not

Satan uses fear to stop us. God uses faith to lift us. Fear and faith are both available to us and by choice we can have either. However, faith and fear don't like to be together. When one is present the other leaves. Belief works with faith; doubt works with fear. If the doubt-n-fear duo take up residence in your home, they probably keep you up at night and follow you around throughout the day. They talk non-stop and commentate on everything you think and do. Worry is nothing more or less than the habit of letting doubt and fear color everything in our lives in various shades of negativity.

God's palette comprises a very different color scheme. Belief and faith are bright. There are no shadows and lurking "gotchas." They don't yammer all the time. Instead, with excellent manners they wait to be invited to speak. Once engaged they are super strong and determined. Yet they are also easily dismissed and will leave if not welcome.

Fear is not your friend. Don't put up with it. Pray for the gift of faith. God will help you turn on this wonderful light and chase away the fear.

I love the song, *How Firm a Foundation*. It's like a personal invitation from God:

"Fear not, I am with thee; oh, be not dismayed, For I am thy God and will still give thee aid. I'll strengthen thee, help thee, and cause thee to stand, Upheld by my righteous, omnipotent hand."

The scriptures mention "Fear of the Lord" which is very different than the worldly fear described above.

"Unlike worldly fear that creates alarm and anxiety, godly fear is a source of peace, assurance, and confidence. But how can anything associated with fear be...helpful? The righteous fear I am [describing] encompasses a deep feeling of reverence, respect, and awe for the Lord Jesus Christ [and] obedience to His commandments..." (David A. Bednar, "Therefore They Hushed Their Fears," *Ensign*, May 2015)

Turn off the noise of the world

We might ask, "why the constant bombardment of thoughts, words, and ideas from the wrong side when that's not what I want?" Like a constant radio or Wi-Fi signal, both light and dark are always broadcasting. Where ever we go in life, we face clever marketing designed to attract and move us. Satan takes the in-your-face-all-the-time approach to recruiting. As in the poem by Alexander Pope, he wears you down:

**"Vice is a monster of so frightful mien
As to be hated needs but to be seen;
Yet seen too oft, familiar with her face,
We first endure, then pity, then embrace."**

Years ago, I was in California at a conference for entrepreneurs. I don't remember who the speaker was but he said something like, "if you don't want to be

"The more we incline our hearts and minds toward God, the more heavenly light distills upon our souls. And each time we willingly and earnestly seek that light, we indicate to God our readiness to receive more light. Gradually, things that before seemed hazy, dark, and remote become clear, bright, and familiar to us.

"By the same token, if we remove ourselves from the light of the gospel, our own light begins to dim—not in a day or a week but gradually over time—until we look back and can't quite understand why we had ever believed the gospel was true. Our previous knowledge might even seem foolish to us because what once was so clear has again become blurred, hazy, and distant." Dieter F. Uchtdorf, "Receiving a Testimony of Light and Truth," *Ensign*, November 2014 poor, find out what the poor people are reading and stop reading it!" That same concept applies to personal revelation. All around us are those seeking happiness in places that are incapable of delivering what they want. Each of us has familiar habits and addictions. Like an old song stuck on replay, we listen to it over and over even after we're bored with it. Our habits and addictions work to keep us stuck in energy-sapping, life sucking ruts and dead ends.

If your relationship with God is "poor," find out what people without God in their lives are reading, watching, listening to and doing and consider removing those things from your life in whole or in part.

One of the best questions you can ask yourself is, "What do I desire to have revealed to me today?" Take some time with this and clarify what you want. If you don't decide, who will? There's an old saying: If you don't stand for something, you'll fall for anything. And that's exactly what's happening. Most people run on default mode, going wherever the wind blows them. They don't realize they are falling for habits that keep them small and trapped.

If there were no limits to what you could know and receive, what would you want to know and receive? There are limitless revelations to

> "Cease to be idle; cease to be unclean; cease to find fault one with another; cease to sleep longer than is needful; retire to thy bed early, that ye may not be weary; arise early, that your bodies and your minds may be invigorated." D&C 88:124

pursue which are spread across a vast spectrum from the world's limited knowledge to God's infinite knowledge. Modern technologies like the Internet make it possible for us to be completely consumed with information, and entertainment of every sort. In fact, there is now more content created and placed online throughout the world everyday than what can be consumed in a lifetime.

Like it or not, you choose patterns every day that compound to your betterment or detriment. There is no longer any such thing as *not deciding*. "The Internet...records your desires, expressed in the form of searches and clicks. There are legions waiting to fill those desires. As you surf the Internet, you leave tracks—what you communicate, where you have been, how long you have been there, and the kinds of things that interest you. In this way, the Internet creates a cyber profile for you—in a sense, your 'cyber book of life.' As in life, the Internet will give you more and more of what you seek. If your desires are pure, the Internet can magnify them, making it ever easier to engage in worthy pursuits. But the opposite is also true" (Randall L. Ridd "The Choice Generation" *Ensign,* May 2014).

In order to hear the voice of God, you must turn on more of the God-channels and turn down the world's noise. This is no small thing. If you're like me, you have addictions to worldly content. Habits don't turn on and off in a day. But clear intent coupled with persistence can change anything. It's not that you must stop wanting everything you're familiar with; it's more that you must cultivate the desire for something even better.

Several years ago, I finally admitted to myself I was eating too much and didn't know how to eat less. Of course I "knew" this had been going on for a long time, but there's a difference between knowing something and being willing to do something about it. One day it hit me that I just needed to be stronger than the next bite of food. I wasn't strong enough yet to take on the whole plate but if I focused on a single bite I could battle that and win. My body needs food and I have the responsibility to nurture my body rather than fight against it. (After all, my spirit and body are going to get to be together forever after the resurrection so I might as well make friends and get along!) With regard to eating, my body not my spirit was the master and this needed to change for both our sakes.

Instead of plowing through a plate of food with the voraciousness of a sixth child in a household of nine kids—mostly boys—who knew that seconds depended on swallowing fast, I needed to take a step back and breathe. The Lord helped me—and is helping me—to take each bite one at a time with a little pause of gratitude between each fork full so that I have the chance to stop at the "sufficient" bite. What a difference this has made!

This same process can apply to any area where we find the body has taken control and we want our spirit to regain control. We might be over-consuming social media, video or online games, news feeds, weather channels, sports and their endless pre and post-game analysis, posting or chatting or pinning or wandering, etc... It's very difficult to eliminate something from our life without first finding its replacement. Our time defaults to the lowest common denominator, even to a full vegetative state of mind if we are not purposeful with it. So start by adding in more God-channels; add more minutes for God-time each day. In the beginning, it can be a fight to not go where you've been going and the new thing you "want" might seem much less interesting than what you've been familiar with.

Please don't try to keep all the world time you've got going while adding in the incremental God-time. This will only make you more tired than you already are and weaken you to where the defaults have more power than your desires to change. I started getting up earlier in the morning when it is usually quieter and I'm more rested. At first I made the mistake of not going to bed earlier on the other end and this made it tougher to establish a new God-centric morning routine. I had the habit of going to bed late which sabotaged me.

> "Don't yield to Satan's lie that you don't have time to study the scriptures. Choose to take time to study them. Feasting on the word of God each day is more important than sleep, school, work, television shows, video games, or social media. You may need to reorganize your priorities to provide time for the study of the word of God. If so, do it! ... I testify that as we actively come unto Him, we can endure every temptation, every heartache, every challenge we face." Richard G. Scott, "Make the Exercise of Faith Your First Priority," *Ensign*, November 2014

If you want conversations with God about things that matter more than anything in this world you've got to choose better sources for your constant personal revelation. Whatever you surround yourself with—intentionally or not—impacts the quality of your personal revelations and whether they be of God or of man or a confusing mix of the two.

> "What we insistently desire, over time, is what we will eventually become and what we will receive in eternity. ...
>
> "... Only by educating and training our desires can they become our allies instead of our enemies!"
>
> Neal A. Maxwell, "According to the Desire of [Our] Hearts," *Ensign,* Nov. 1996

Avoid doubts and second guessing

Opposition is a part of the journey. The forces of good and evil compete for your attention and allegiance. "There is no neutral ground in the universe. Every square inch, every split second is claimed by God, and counterclaimed by Satan." (C.S. Lewis) Therefore, you can only expect the devil will shout his arguments for why the things of God are unreasonable and flawed.

Discerning which voice is providing the personal revelation can be challenging. Mistakes and missteps are part of the journey. Waiting to take a step until it can be a perfect step will keep you forever at the starting block. Satan does not want you to tune him out; he's spent too much time and effort already to let you go easily. That's why he wrestles with your mind, alerting you to fictitious dangers

"Some might ask, 'But what about my doubts?'

"It's natural to have questions—the acorn of honest inquiry has often sprouted and matured into a great oak of understanding. There are few members of the Church who, at one time or another, have not wrestled with serious or sensitive questions. One of the purposes of the Church is to nurture and cultivate the seed of faith—even in the sometimes sandy soil of doubt and uncertainty. Faith is to hope for things which are not seen but which are true.

"Therefore, my dear brothers and sisters—my dear friends—please, first doubt your doubts before you doubt your faith. We must never allow doubt to hold us prisoner and keep us from the divine love, peace, and gifts that come through faith in the Lord Jesus Christ." Dieter F. Uchtdorf, "Come, Join With Us," *Ensign,* November 2013

that await in your quest for greater light and knowledge from God. He takes cheap shots and stoops to borrowing scriptures out of context to confuse and reason with you.

In reality he's been running you into the ditch of doubt your whole life. If you want to spend more time on the highway of happiness and less time in the ditch, don't give in to the devil's trickery. He wants you to think that you can't get on or stay on the highway so you shouldn't even try.

Look, you're going to run into ditches and career off course from time to time, maybe even a lot of the time. The good news is that because of Christ, you don't have to stay in the ditch. You can be rescued every time. In fact it's rather uncanny how the tow truck is always close by to pull you out...as if God saw it coming and already prepared to help you.

The reason you come to trust God is because you come to realize He never lets you down. It's just the opposite with Satan—he always seeks to destroy and diminish. Herein lies part of how you grow in confidence that the voice you are listening to is the right voice. Notice the patterns that each consistently follows.

"For behold, the Spirit of Christ is given to every man, that he may know good from evil; wherefore, I show unto you the way to judge; for every thing which inviteth to do good, and to persuade to believe in Christ, is sent forth by the power and gift of Christ; wherefore ye may know with a perfect knowledge it is of God.

"But whatsoever thing persuadeth men to do evil, and believe not in Christ, and deny him, and serve not God, then ye may know with a perfect knowledge it is of the devil; for after this manner doth the devil work, for he persuadeth no man to do good, no, not one; neither do his angels; neither do they who subject themselves unto him." Moroni 7:16-17

The following table gives some examples of patterns you may start to notice as you learn to discern:

List A: Revelations from God and His servants	List B: Revelations from Satan and his servants
Inspire courage, confidence, hope and belief	Inspire fear, worry, and doubt
Align with "Golden Rule": Win/win	Involve losing: Win/lose or lose/lose
Tend to be positive and encouraging	Tend to be negative and discouraging
Tend to help focus outward and on the long term	Tend to be focused inward and on the short term
Tend to come when we ask and are seeking	Come without effort like a constant barrage of critical and criticizing dialogues in our head
Give us energy and desire to change and repent	Suck energy and make us feel stuck
Invite a can-do, things will work out, keep going kind of attitude	Insist on a can't do, things never work for me, might as well quit kind of attitude
Invite virtuous, kind, forgiving, loving thoughts and actions	Tempt to self-gratification, lust, un-kindness, hatred, envy, bitterness, greed, etc...
Warn of dangers; give instructions, help, commandments, and counsel for safety	Lull into a false sense of security, apathy, and lethargy
Reveal and confirm the truth	Mislead and distract
Invite abundant thinking (e.g. there's enough and to spare so you can share)	Create scarcity thinking (e.g. always a lack—so grab yours before it's too late or runs out)

Look for the patterns taught by God's revelations—you find what you look for. This is a key to shifting away from revelations that hurt (List B) toward revelations that help (List A).

Be purposeful. When negative revelations hit you (List B), ask God specifically for a personal message from His side (List A). As you do, your confidence grows and diminishes second guessing.

> "The purpose of my remarks is to proclaim the joyful message that God Himself—the Lord of Hosts who knows all truth—has given His children the promise that they can know truth for themselves. ... The Everlasting and Almighty God, the Creator of this vast universe, will speak to those who approach Him with a sincere heart and real intent. He will speak to them in dreams, visions, thoughts, and feelings. He will speak in a way that is unmistakable and that transcends human experience. He will give them divine direction and answers for their personal lives... God cares about you. He will listen, and He will answer your personal questions. The answers to your prayers will come in His own way and in His own time, and therefore, you need to learn to listen to His voice." Dieter F. Uchtdorf, "Receiving a Testimony of Light and Truth," *Ensign*, November 2014

One-word answers or feelings or pictures are ok

Some of the most life changing moments I've had with God involved very short answers and revelations.

<u>Example of a yes/no answer</u>: Nearly 10 years ago, I came to a crossroads and needed urgent directional help. I thought about the best options and came up with two that made sense. This was not a casual, anything-could-work kind of moment. We were in the middle of a family crisis and I had just resigned from my executive position at work.

I went to a quiet place where I couldn't be interrupted and basically told the Lord I needed serious help and would stay as long as it took. And it took a while. I presented the best plan I could think of regarding next employment and asked Him to confirm it was right. Nothing. I tried again. Still nothing. So I went to my second option thinking it must be that. Nothing again. Repeating options one and two only brought the faint emergence of a third possibility that honestly I wanted nothing to do with.

Desperate times call for desperate measures so I allowed myself to bring this unwanted third choice onto stage. Almost immediately I felt a confirming feeling that this was right. That's not what I had wanted so I asked again and again with the same result: warm, good feeling that this was right. I asked Father, "Are you telling me 'yes?'" To which the *yes* sensation came again. "Ok, Father, I just heard a 'yes', is that correct?" Yes.

And so I did that option, not because it's what I had wanted or even before considered, but because that sincere prayer was about finding out God's will and doing it no matter what. I learned an important, life changing lesson that day. You can get help in *any* area you need or want in life if you're willing to be serious enough about it to ask with a faith stronger than your desire to do things your way.

There were times after that day I went to get answers in a more casual, less sincere way and came away empty handed. Be sincere. Don't take it for granted. It's not difficult. It just needs to be real.

Example of a short revelation: Fast forward about three years and I stood at another significant moment feeling severe stress and wanting relief, a change from what I was doing that seemed to be sucking me dry with very little to show for it. Again I went to spend time with the Lord away from the noise of the world and do whatever it took, however long it took to get the go ahead to take a new direction.

After some time in quiet prayer and pleading, I received the clearest prompting/revelation I ever remember getting that came as a thought that was almost audible in my head, "Stay the course; the way and the means will be provided." These words—so direct—surprised me. I asked the Lord, did You just tell me …?" and I repeated back to Him what I had felt/heard. And He immediately confirmed the words with the *yes* sensation with which I was now very familiar and trusted.

This experience not only kept me going when I wanted to quit, it taught me personally that the Lord really does see everything past, present, and future. He will help us go around, under, over or through any obstacle that may stand in the way of the best plans He has for us. Sometimes He does have us take a different course. That time He instructed me to "stay the course." And certainly He was right in ways I could never have known, that weren't fully evident until several more years passed.

Communication with God is not about getting page after page of recorded dialog. It's about having a relationship, the most important relationship! How God speaks with you and what your conversations are like may be different than how He talks with me. That's ok. I'm not you. God is interested in *you*. What matters to you, matters to Him. The more time you spend with Him in ways that work for you, the more you will discover what matters to Him. The more what-you-want-for-you

"We see such a limited part of the eternal plan He has fashioned for each one of us. Trust Him, even when in eternal perspective it temporarily hurts very much. Have patience when you are asked to wait when you want immediate action. He may ask you to do things which are powerfully against your will. Exercise faith and say, Let Thy will be done. Such experiences, honorably met, prepare you and condition you for yet greater blessings. As your Father, His purpose is your eternal happiness, your continuing development, your increasing capacity. ... You may not always know why He does what He does, but you can know that He is perfectly just and perfectly merciful. He would have you suffer no consequence, no challenge, endure no burden that is superfluous to your good."
Richard G. Scott, "Obtaining Help from the Lord," *Ensign*, Nov. 1991

matches up with what God wants for you, the more peace, happiness, and joy you will find in this life. You'll also look forward more to returning to His presence and progressing eternally.

God may communicate with you more in pictures. This could include dreams or visions while you are asleep or awake. He is willing to engage with you in one or more ways that work for you. I can't even count the number of times I have prayed asking God to give me answers in a way I could understand.

Years ago, a company I worked for hit a financial crisis. I felt trapped with no way out. One morning, immediately as I got out of bed, a familiar song—a hymn—played spontaneously in my mind. The song gave me what I needed to get through that day. The next morning, same thing, only this time it was a different song with a different message that was perfect again for the needs of that day. This went on for about a month every day, right when I woke up; different songs, always starting at a perfect spot in a verse or chorus to deliver the precise gift I needed to keep going. This tender mercy from God ended the day after the problem at work resolved and I no longer needed it to survive.

You may have a way you think would work for you to get answers, even if that way doesn't make sense to others. If so, ask God if he would help you get answers in that specific way. If not, ask for help learning a way that could work for you. Just as we experience the physical world through our senses of sight, hearing, touch, smell, and taste so we may experience communication with God through our physical senses and our spiritual senses. Our spirits are much older and mature than our physical bodies so there are times that we feel or sense things our mortal bodies cannot comprehend. (see Appendix: Examples of personal revelations that have encouraged me—March 30, 2014)

Often described as feelings, our communications can come in bursts of understanding or even a knowing beyond our ability to explain. Still it may be even more real than what we discern with our lesser physical senses. The important thing to remember here is that communication with God can be simple and easy. He wants to visit with us: "Behold, I stand at the door, and knock: if any man hear my voice, and open the door, I will come in to him, and will sup with him, and he with me." Revelation 3:20

"Wo be unto him that shall say:

We have received the word of God,

and we need no more of the word of God, for we have

enough!

"For behold, thus saith the Lord God:

I will give unto the children of men line upon line,

precept upon precept,

here a little and there a little;

and blessed are those who hearken unto my precepts,

and lend an ear unto my counsel,

for they shall learn wisdom;

for unto him that receiveth I will give more;

and from them that shall say, We have enough,

from them shall be taken away even that which they have.

"Cursed is he that putteth his trust in man,

or maketh flesh his arm,

or shall hearken unto the precepts of men,

save their precepts shall be given by the power of the Holy

Ghost."

2 Nephi 28:29-31

"...remember, remember that it is upon the rock of our Redeemer, who is Christ, the Son of God, that ye must build your foundation; that when the devil shall send forth his mighty winds, yea, his shafts in the whirlwind, yea, when all his hail and his mighty storm shall beat upon you, it shall have no power over you to drag you down to the gulf of misery and endless wo, because of the rock upon which ye are built, which is a sure foundation, a foundation whereon if men build they cannot fall."

Helaman 5:12

Continue
Keep wanting it!
Persist!
Be obedient!
Harness the power of forgiveness

PART 3: CONTINUE

Keep wanting it!

For some odd reason, we tend to stop doing things that work. Communicating with God is no exception. When we face difficulty or are overwhelmed in any way, we open up to receive help. When we hurt and cry out for help, we get help. On the other hand, when the crisis passes the urgency is gone. Unless another trial comes quickly, the craving-for-help like a hunger is satisfied and we revert back to the way things were. This reality helps us see we have a choice to:

(1) maintain things as they currently are or

(2) go beyond the limits of our comfort zone and expand our previous capacity.

Let's briefly look at each of these:

Maintain things as they currently are

Let's say that I live in a tent; that's the life I know. It's crowded to be sure but I'm familiar with it, so that's ok. Assume a storm comes through. It knocks down my tent and causes some damage to the fabric or the tent poles. Suddenly I'm in crisis, clearly outside the boundaries of my comfort zone. Feeling overwhelmed by this problem, I urgently pray and ask for help because I don't know how to fix damaged tent poles or fabric. I believe He will help me because there is no other alternative and I have nowhere else to turn. I get help to fix things back to the way they were, back to where I was comfortable or at least back to the familiar where I knew how to cope and exist.

Go beyond the limits of our comfort zone and expand our previous capacity

Same tent situation, same storm, same crisis—I'm suddenly outside of my comfort zone needing help and urgently seeking help. I get the help I asked for but instead of just using God's hand temporarily, I wake up and see a new possibility. If God can help me in crisis and give me what I ask for in restoring my crude existence in a tent, what if I didn't stop asking Him for help? What if I came to Him and said something like: "Thank You for helping me and I'm grateful for the tent. I just saw You do something I couldn't do by myself and it was amazing to see Thy hand. I don't really want to stay forever in a tent. I've heard about homes where life can be even better with less stress and more comforts. I know that since You have power to create flowers and trees and mountains and worlds, there's no limit to what you can do. Will you help me to get a home?" So instead of going out of my comfort zone and right back into it to stay, I glimpse a higher plan. The trial of the storm can encourage me to move to a better place if I'm willing to call upon the Lord. He can guide me on a journey instead of just help me get back to where I was.

Here's where most get stuck. Without the focus of a clear, compelling objective, we won't make the effort to continue calling upon the Lord to do amazing things. In this way, trials are a *huge* blessing because they compel us to keep seeking God and asking for His help, which builds our faith and trust in Him. Without trials, it's easy to get complacent and see communication with God as unnecessary. This wouldn't be problematic except that this world is the equivalent of a tent. There's infinitely more to our existence than what this world has to offer. If our obsession is only to maintain our tent or get bigger, better, fancier stuff here, we are settling for a crumb when God is willing to give us endless loaves of bread.

In a very real sense, we need to be dissatisfied with the world and its enticing array of superficiality. Obedience to God's commandments needs to be a quest no matter our circumstances. The more we communicate with Him, the more we become aware of our nothingness compared to Him. To seek for divine attributes such as love, forgiveness, gratitude, kindness, charity is not trivial. Until our craving for godliness becomes as compelling as our need for help when in "tent crisis" we settle for far less than God is willing to give us.

Communication with God means interaction with an exalted being who constantly expands in glory and light. When His light shines on the darkness around us, we have the choice to continue toward the mansions He has prepared for us or retreat back to our tents and avoid eye contact with Him lest He invite us to higher ground. (Because then we'd have to move and move and move forward, continually getting comfortable being uncomfortable, because that is what growth requires.)

One way you can gauge if you are in tent mode or growth mode is to examine how you feel about repentance. If repentance feels like a burden to be carried only occasionally and obedience is a chore just to keep you from needing repentance too often, then you are in tent mode. If on the other hand, repentance is a yoke you've taken upon you as one desiring to follow Christ forever and to rely on Him forever and you love it and rejoice in it, then you are in growth mode.

Tent mode = hard to sustain communication with God

Growth mode = communication with God is an essential part of your daily walk and gets easier and easier as His voice and power in your life get more and more familiar.

Persist!

Developing new habits and letting go of old patterns takes time. Even if you *really* want better results, new knowledge or greater understanding; even if you're *really* willing to change—growth takes time.

Sometimes there is an inverse relationship between work required and results that can be expected. If I plant a fruit tree from seed today, I won't get any fruit from that tree for three to nine years, depending on the type or variety of fruit tree. It also takes more effort to nurture a young tree than it takes to care for the mature tree which by then is yielding abundant fruit.

"And behold, as the tree beginneth to grow, ye will say: Let us nourish it with great care, that it may get root, that it may grow up, and bring forth fruit unto us. And now behold, if ye nourish it with much care it will get root, and grow up, and bring forth fruit.

"But if ye neglect the tree, and take no thought for its nourishment, behold it will not get any root; and when the heat of the sun cometh and scorcheth it, because it hath no root it withers away, and ye pluck it up and cast it out.

"Now, this is not because the seed was not good, neither is it because the fruit thereof would not be desirable; but it is because
your ground is barren, and ye will not nourish the tree, therefore ye cannot have the fruit thereof.

"And thus, if ye will not nourish the word, looking forward with an eye of faith to the fruit thereof, ye can never pluck of the fruit of the tree of life.

"But if ye will nourish the

"Each family prayer, each episode of family scripture study, and each family home evening is a brushstroke on the canvas of our souls. No one event may appear to be very impressive or memorable. But just as the yellow and gold and brown strokes of paint complement each other and produce an impressive masterpiece, so our consistency in doing seemingly small things can lead to significant spiritual results" David A. Bednar,"More Diligent and Concerned at Home," *Ensign*, November 2009

word, yea, nourish the tree as it beginneth to grow, by your faith with great diligence, and with patience, looking forward to the fruit thereof, it shall take root; and behold it shall be a tree springing up unto everlasting life." Alma 32:37-41

According to an old proverb, "The best time to plant a tree is twenty years ago; the second best time is today." The sooner you get started, the sooner you can enjoy the promised fruits. Getting started and staying motivated can be the hardest part when there is delayed gratification. Not surprisingly then, many do not stay the course long enough to receive the reward.

God understands how difficult this can be for His children. He prepared a way by faith for us to receive His word throughout our lives even while we learn to communicate with Him in more personal ways. The words of His prophets in both ancient and modern scriptures are one way we can have immediate access to His revelations. We learn how to apply these revelations to our own situations through study, practice, and becoming very familiar with the stories and parables provided.

"Wherefore... feast upon the words of Christ; for behold, the words of Christ will tell you all things what ye should do. ...if ye cannot understand them it will be because ye ask not, neither do ye knock; wherefore, ye are not brought into the light, but must perish in the dark."
2 Nephi 32:3-4

If at first you are more familiar with the language of the world than with the language of God, don't lose heart or give up. Keep asking, keep seeking, and keep knocking. Some ask why it can be so hard at times. Fortunately, there is a divine purpose for opposition as it can strengthen us and give us understanding we could gain in no other way.

"For it must needs be, that there is an opposition in all things. If not so, ... righteousness could not be brought to pass, neither wickedness, neither holiness nor misery, neither good nor bad. Wherefore, all things must needs be a compound in one; wherefore, if it should be one body it must needs remain as dead, having no life neither death, nor corruption nor incorruption, happiness nor misery, neither sense nor insensibility." 2 Nephi 2:11

If it took two years, five years, ten years...or a life time to learn how to talk with God, would it be worth it? Would you do it? Only you as the tree farmer of your soul can answer that question. This is certain: if you persist in your quest to receive more light, more understanding, more personal revelation from God, He will bless you and provide the way for you to get what you really want and to enjoy greater success in the things that matter most in this life and in the Life to come.

"...I, Nephi, was desirous also that I might see, and hear, and know of these things, by the power of the Holy Ghost, which is the gift of God unto all those who diligently seek him, as well in times of old as in the time that he should manifest himself unto the children of men.

"For he is the same yesterday, today, and forever; and the way is prepared for all men from the foundation of the world, if it so be that they repent and come unto him.

"For he that diligently seeketh shall find; and the mysteries of God shall be unfolded unto them, by the power of the Holy Ghost, as well in these times as in times of old, and as well in times of old as in times to come; wherefore, the course of the Lord is one eternal round." 1 Nephi 10:17-19

Be Obedient!

Receiving more abundantly requires faithfulness and diligence in respecting what has already been received. This makes sense. Why give someone more when they're not even using what has already been granted.

> "The Lord has the power to bless us at any time. Yet we see that to count on His help, we must consistently obey His commandments." Richard G. Scott, "Obtaining Help from the Lord," *Ensign*, November 1991

President Ezra Taft Benson said it best: "When obedience ceases to be an irritant and becomes our quest, in that moment God will endow us with power."

One of the great stories in the Book of Mormon involves the ever diligent Nephi growing weary with his older brothers' tendency to struggle with patterns of disobedience that impacted their ability to keep pace.

"... I spake unto my brethren, desiring to know of them the cause of their disputations.

"And they said: Behold, we cannot understand the words which our father hath spoken...

"And I said unto them: Have ye inquired of the Lord?

"And they said unto me: We have not; for the Lord maketh no such thing known unto us.

"Behold, I said unto them: How is it that ye do not keep the commandments of the Lord? How is it that ye will perish, because of the hardness of your hearts?

"Do ye not remember the things which the Lord hath said?—If ye will not harden your hearts, and ask me in faith, believing that ye shall receive, with diligence in keeping my commandments, surely these things shall be made known unto you." 1 Nephi 15:6-11

If you feel a bit like Nephi's brothers when they said "the Lord maketh no such thing known unto us," take heart. Nephi also struggled at times with obedience like we all do (see 2 Nephi 4:17-19). Please don't give up. Nephi had to persist. So must we. Keep working at it.

> "I was trying to make my mouth SAY I would do the right thing and the clean thing...but deep down in me I knowed it was a lie, and He knowed it. You can't pray a lie—I found that out." Mark Twain, *The Adventures of Huckleberry Finn*, Ch 31:P3

From this story we learn that revelation from God is impacted by how we respond to what He tells us. If we are willing to obey God's word to us through His servants, then when we want to know things for ourselves we can go with confidence before the Lord and expect to have a more believable, credible interaction.

Harness the power of forgiveness

The Bible is full of stories that inspire and instruct. Some are much more familiar than others probably due to a sensational factor. Stories like Noah's ark or the parting of the Red Sea can easily be told or even made into interesting movies. Yet some of the "lesser" stories contain valuable insights we can look to as we face important daily challenges less dramatic than fleeing a pursuing army of Egyptians.

One such story involves a conflict described in 1 Samuel 25 between David and Nabal. In short, David made what he considered to be a reasonable, deserving request and was rebuffed. This made David very angry. Nabal was "clearly" in the wrong and must pay for his grievous misdeed. Nabal's wife, Abigail, heard about the incident after the fact including that David was on his way with a large group of men with swords to fight.

Abigail sprang into action, loaded provisions on the backs of several donkeys and hurried to meet David and his little army. As they met up, Abigail "fell at [David's] feet, and said, 'Upon me, my lord, upon me let this iniquity be; and let thine handmaid, I pray thee, speak in thine audience, and hear the words of thine handmaid. I pray thee, forgive the trespass of thine handmaid.'" 1 Samuel 24, 28. These verses illustrate the idea of someone who has no fault standing in the place of another. In this case, David forgave Abigail on behalf of Nabal which avoided great devastation.

This idea of intercession is not new except we usually think only of the intercession Christ makes between us and our Heavenly Father. Christ paid the price of our sins and therefore is able to settle our debts with God. What if intercession could likewise be made between people on

Earth such as was done by Abigail? She literally took upon herself the sins of her husband and came before David as if she was the debtor. She owned the wrong doing, paid for it, and sought forgiveness as if she had done the wrong herself. Can it be that Christ's atoning intercession, in like manner, goes beyond reconciling us to God and covers the common disputes between people here on Earth?

How often do we face misunderstandings, hurt feelings, betrayal, or any of a host of injustices that weigh us down and weaken us into a victim state? While we wallow in the role of victim, life is literally drained away from us. The remedy is forgiveness.

Knowing this, God gave us the commandment to forgive by saying, "I the Lord, will forgive whom I will forgive, but of you it is required to forgive all men." D&C 64:10

The source of one's personal revelation is deeply impacted by what we hold on to. Bad things, challenging things, abusive things, trying things, accidents, mishaps, evil...all of us are impacted by the world in which we live— a place described as lost

> "I wish today to speak of forgiveness. I think it may be the greatest virtue on earth, and certainly the most needed. There is so great a need for... forgiveness. It is the great principle emphasized in all of scripture, both ancient and modern.
>
> ...
>
> "Somehow forgiveness, with love and tolerance, accomplishes miracles that can happen in no other way." Gordon B. Hinckley, "Forgiveness," Ensign, Nov. 2005

and fallen. Part of the test of mortality is to face opportunities to grow in their many, varied forms. What will we choose? How will we respond? Will we learn to choose the good instead of the bad? Will we persist or give up? The world seeks to scare us into submission to fear, worry, and doubt; or lull us away from truth into dead end paths whose entrances falsely present expected outcomes. Despite such extraordinary opposition, this life is a magnificent blessing as it helps us develop faith and virtue. (see APPENDIX: Examples of personal revelations that have encouraged me: Friday, January 10, 2014)

As hurts so easily give way to frustration and bitterness, the sooner we stop the internal bleeding of blame the better. When someone is badly injured, the first priority is to save their life rather than waste any time debating the cause(s). If the injury is noticeably physical, we tend to administer first aid more readily than in cases where the injury is spiritual, emotional, or psychological. In these latter cases, the norm is to stew, and brew, and compound the fracture by breeding soul-toxins of every sort imaginable. Satan's laboratory is open 24/7 and he loves to share his favorite recipes. His most common ingredients include self-pity, anger, gossip, storytelling, pride, justification, bitterness, and hatred. Some of these take time to fabricate and turn out best when simmered on low heat.

Forgiveness should be the biggest and most used bottle in the medicine cabinet, applied liberally to others as well as to ourselves. It's one of those prescriptions that always works and never runs out, yet it never seems to be used as often as instructed on the label given by the Great Physician.

I'm learning that the atonement of Christ is much more encompassing than I previously imagined. His intercession works not just between us and God but between us and other people. If God looks to His Son and respects the price paid on our behalf, can we not do the same by looking to Christ when we are filing our grievances? If God cannot see or remember our sins because Christ is standing in the way, what if we saw Christ instead of the perpetrator? What if like Abigail in the Bible we let Christ own the wrong-doing? Then like David, forgive the intermediary when at first it may have been too hard to forgive the "Nabal" directly?

Forgive quickly; forgive often. Forgive when you can; forgive when you can't. If at first the injury is just too great to forgive directly, let Christ step in with His limitless, atoning resources and "purchase the offenses" along with the obligations that go with the offenses. Then Christ, as the new "owner" of the offenses, can look you in the eye and ask you to forgive Him. If you find it somewhat uncomfortable to be asked to forgive Christ when He is the one that makes it possible for your own sins to be forgiven, simply say "of course, I forgive you; I should be asking forgiveness of You." And now you've got it about right!

When we see how many debts Christ has borne and settled on our behalf—especially His ransom payments to spring us free from the prisons of sin—it's easier to allow Him to provide that same service for those we think owe

55

us. So forgive others or forgive Christ standing in for others. Forgive yourself or forgive Christ standing in for you. Trust His power to stop the bleeding, start the healing and make things right that could have never been made right without Him.

If all debts were run through the single clearing house or bank of Christ, what devastation and further injury would be avoided! Christ's bank is unlike any other—our personal debts cleared off the books are always greater than what we are owed. We always come out ahead! Christ's eternal resources—His infinite atonement—fund the clearing house and all are invited to come and partake liberally. Just remember to show at the door your membership card called forgiveness!

"Ho, every one that thirsteth, come ye to the waters, and he that hath no money; come ye, buy, and eat; yea, come, buy wine and milk without money and without price."
Isaiah 55:1

Communication with God is so much easier when we're not stepping over and around the debris of unresolved grievances. Such clutter invites revelation from darkness. If your efforts to talk with God are being met with static or too much bitter-chatter, forgive away the junk that may be blocking those heavenly passage ways.

SUMMARY

God lives and is interested in you! You can have a personal, ongoing relationship with Him by following the simple steps outlined above. God wants to talk to you. He wants to be a part of your life. Each of us has wonderful opportunities right in front of us to hear God's voice and even have conversations with Him. God will meet you where you are and speak in a language you can understand.

In a world full of noise and clever distractions, it's easy to get caught up in the clamor of urgent, lesser things. Everyone rushes here or there to satisfy the demands of work and pleasure. If you're caught up like a squirrel in an exercise wheel, running fast but not really going anywhere, it's difficult to imagine adding one more thing. However, the idea is to do less of what's not working and more of what will.

Turning off familiar voices working against you in order to receive more of God's voice will turn personal revelation into a help rather than a hindrance. No matter where you are in life, no matter how things look on the outside or feel on the inside, know that you matter. You have eternal worth. However much you are or aren't asking and receiving, you can ask for and receive more.

Starting can be the hardest part of any journey. Procrastination only gives more time for additional concrete of excuses to be poured all around you. Being stuck is not what you want. What's more, it's completely unnecessary.

If talking with God is important to you—or you want it to become important—here's a summary of the sections and steps discussed above that will help you in your quest:

Begin	Improve	Continue
Decide you want to talk with Him	Be patient with yourself	Keep wanting it!
Desire it!	Be grateful	Persist!
Become familiar with God's voice	Choose to believe	Be obedient!
Talk to Him like a normal person	Fear not	Harness the power of forgiveness
Write your prayers to Him and record His responses	Turn off the noise of the world	
Ask Him questions	Avoid doubts and second guessing	
Don't be afraid to talk with Him	One-word answers or feelings or pictures are ok	
Keep it simple		

Begin today! Improve as you go! And don't stop—keep going! You can do it! You can talk *with* God!

"There are many listening today who feel a pressing need for that blessing of personal revelation from our loving Heavenly Father. … We all know that human judgment and logical thinking will not be enough to get answers to the questions that matter most in life. We need revelation from God. And we will need not just one revelation in a time of stress, but we need a constantly renewed stream. We need not just one flash of light and comfort, but we need the continuing blessing of communication with God. … God pours out revelation, through the Holy Ghost, on His children." Henry B. Eyring, "Continuing Revelation," *Ensign*, November 2014

APPENDIX

Ask, and ye shall receive

This whole section is simply a reference place to begin listing examples of the times and ways God has asked us to ask Him so we can receive more from Him. As one of God's modern prophets once said, "No message appears in scripture more times, in more ways than, 'Ask, and ye shall receive.'" Boyd K. Packer, "Reverence Invites Revelation," *Ensign*, November 1991

Here's the list I started just from searching key words. I add to the list when I come across more scriptural references that tie into this theme. Please add to this list for yourself in your own study. Have confidence that God is always inviting you to come and interact with Him as you have needs, desires, or just want to know things.

"If ye abide in me, and my words abide in you, ye shall ask what ye will, and it shall be done unto you." John 15:7

"Therefore, ask, and ye shall receive; knock, and it shall be opened unto you; for he that asketh, receiveth; and unto him that knocketh, it shall be opened. John 16:24

"Seek unto my Father, and it shall be done in that very moment what ye shall ask, if ye ask in faith, believing that ye shall receive." JST, Mark 9:45

"If any of you lack wisdom, let him ask of God, that giveth to all *men* liberally, and upbraideth not; and it shall be given him." James 1:5

"Ye ask, and receive not, because ye ask amiss." James 4:3

"Behold, you have not understood; you have supposed that I would give it unto you, when you took no thought save it was to ask me." D&C 9:7

"And whatsoever we ask, we receive of him, *because we keep his commandments,* and do those things that are pleasing in his sight." 1 Jn. 3:22; italics added

"Do ye not remember the things which the Lord hath said?—If ye will *not harden your hearts,* and *ask me in faith,* believing that ye shall receive, *with diligence in keeping my commandments,* surely these things shall be made known unto you." 1 Ne. 15:11; italics added

"Wherefore, now after I have spoken these words, if ye cannot understand them it will be because ye ask not, neither do ye knock; wherefore, ye are not brought into the light, but must perish in the dark." 2 Nephi 32:4

"Remember that without faith you can do nothing; therefore *ask in faith. Trifle not* with these things; do not ask for that which you ought not." D&C 8:10; italics added

"If ye are purified and cleansed from all sin, ye shall ask whatsoever you will in the name of Jesus and it shall be done. But know this, *it shall be given you what you shall ask.*" D&C 50:29-30; italics added

"And whatsoever ye shall ask the Father in my name, which is right, believing that ye shall receive, behold it shall be given unto you." 3 Nephi 18:20

"Therefore, ask, and ye shall receive; knock, and it shall be opened unto you; for he that asketh, receiveth; and unto him that knocketh, it shall be opened." 3 Nephi 27:29

"Hitherto have ye asked nothing in my name: ask, and ye shall receive, that your joy may be full." John 16:24

"And, as it is written—Whatsoever ye shall ask in faith, being united in prayer according to my command, ye shall receive." D&C 29:6

"And all things, whatsoever ye shall ask in prayer, believing, ye shall receive." Matthew 21:22

"Ask, and ye shall receive; knock, and it shall be opened unto you. Amen." D&C 4:7

"Therefore, if you will ask of me you shall receive; if you will knock it shall be opened unto you." D&C 11:5

"Therefore, if you will ask of me you shall receive; if you will knock it shall be opened unto you." D&C 6:5

"Therefore, if you will ask of me you shall receive; if you will knock it shall be opened unto you." D&C 14:5

"Behold this is my will; ask and ye shall receive; but men do not always do my will." D&C 103:31

"Let them ask and they shall receive, knock and it shall be opened unto them, and be made known from on high, even by the Comforter, whither they shall go." D&C 75:27

"Draw near unto me and I will draw near unto you; seek me diligently and ye shall find me; ask, and ye shall receive; knock, and it shall be opened unto you. "Whatsoever ye ask the Father in my name it shall be given unto you, *that is expedient for you.*" D&C 88:63-64

"... Be patient in affliction. Ask, and ye shall receive; knock, and it shall be opened unto you." D&C 66:9

"Behold, I say unto you, go forth as I have commanded you; repent of all your sins; ask and ye shall receive; knock and it shall be opened unto you." D&C 49:26

"Wherefore, I knowing that the Lord God was able to preserve our records, I cried unto him continually, for he had said unto me: Whatsoever thing ye shall ask in faith, believing that ye shall receive in the name of Christ, ye shall receive it." Enos 1:15

"And when ye shall receive these things, I would exhort you that ye would ask God, the Eternal Father, in the name

of Christ, if these things are not true; and if
ye shall ask with a sincere heart, with real intent, having
faith in Christ, he will manifest the truth of it unto you, by
the power of the Holy Ghost." Moroni 10:4

"And he also said unto him: If thou wilt turn unto me, and
hearken unto my voice, and believe, and repent of all thy
transgressions, and be baptized, even in water, in the
name of mine Only Begotten Son, who is full of grace and
truth, which is Jesus Christ, the only name which shall be
given under heaven, whereby salvation shall come unto
the children of men, ye shall receive the gift of the Holy
Ghost, asking all things in his name, and whatsoever
ye shall ask, it shall be given you." Moses 6:52

"And after that he came men also were saved by faith in
his name; and by faith, they become the sons of God. And
as surely as Christ liveth he spake these words unto our
fathers, saying: Whatsoever thing ye shall ask the Father in
my name, which is good, in faith believing that ye shall
receive, behold, it shall be done unto you." Moroni 7:26

"And now, if God, who has created you, on whom you are
dependent for your lives and for all that ye have and are,
doth grant unto you whatsoever ye ask that is right, in
faith, believing that ye shall receive, O then, how ye ought
to impart of the substance that ye have one to another."
Mosiah 4:21

"Or what man is there of you, whom if his son ask bread,
will he give him a stone?
"Or if he ask a fish, will he give him a serpent?

"If ye then, being evil, know how to give good gifts unto your children, how much more shall your Father which is in heaven give good things to them that ask him?" Matthew 7:9-11

"Or what man is there of you, who, if his son ask bread, will give him a stone?
"Or if he ask a fish, will he give him a serpent?
"If ye then, being evil, know how to give good gifts unto your children, how much more shall your Father who is in heaven give good things to them that ask him?"
3 Nephi 14:9-11

Examples of personal revelations that have encouraged me

When I record my words of gratitude, praise, supplication, heart ache, feelings or expressions of any kind in my prayer journal, *my* words are not highlighted. The words of love, counsel, wisdom and help I receive (and do my best to record), I like to highlight these (e.g. in yellow). All the words of personal revelation highlighted below—**in a different font like this**—came in response to questions I asked on my knees or wrote by hand in a journal or typed in my prayer journal while sitting at the computer. If you are already praying regularly, the language you use to express yourself is exactly what you can continue with and write or type as you desire to expand the usefulness of this wonderful portal of prayer. If you are new to praying or don't pray regularly, that's ok too. Just use language you are familiar with. I like to begin by saying things like:

- Dear Heavenly Father...
- Good morning, Father!
- Thank You for the chance to meet.
- I have a lot on my mind and I'm not sure where to begin...
- Do You have any suggestions for....?
- I'm thinking about... or struggling with... or not sure about...

I like to be respectful so I usually will start any reference to God with a capital letter. Sometimes I also address Him with "Thee" or "Thou" and sometimes I receive His responses with similar "thee" or "thou" language. (Do what feels most appropriate to you. God will speak to you in a way you can understand.) I also like to think of at least three things I'm grateful for and why and share that with Him in the beginning of my prayer dialogue with Him. This helps me get open to receive more from Him rather than feeling stuck that everything in my life is broken and nothing is going my way, etc...

We all have conversations each day and have ways to start and invite conversation. Sometimes I do all the talking and He is a great listener and just lets me talk. Sometimes I talk very little and follow His example of being a good listener. I've learned He has a lot more He's willing to share with me if I'll let Him. Most of my life, I just didn't let him—at least not this abundantly—though I have prayed daily since my childhood.

Knowing what to share has been important to this writing. All personal revelation from God is sacred and should be held in trust as a most precious gift. The examples below are shared by permission from Him who knows all things and is the source of all truth and light. He asked that I share a few examples that might be of help to others as they also seek to improve their communication with Him.

This I know, God is willing to speak in an expressive way with you and in a way you can receive it. He will use words familiar to you in addition to pointing you to His words already recorded and published elsewhere such as in the scriptures. The errors in sentence structure, punctuation, or expression are entirely my own. The feelings, expressions, and knowledge transmitted by the Spirit as He speaks to us are not always easy to put into words or even write or type fast enough. He has great patience with us and does help us to record His messages—His words that are personal to us—in the best way possible for our benefit if we are willing to receive and not get caught up in our own imperfections. After all, we are like little children learning to walk and He helps us get up each time we fall and encourages us to stand even in the face of regular stumbling.

Please remember the following examples are personal to me. They are not intended to be instructions or commandments to anyone else. If these examples in any way provide ideas or encouragement to you to ASK more, SEEK more, or KNOCK more with confidence that you will RECEIVE more, FIND more, and have more things OPENED to you then I am very happy for you and excited for what awaits you!

This was a pivotal revelation for me. I followed this counsel to come to Him first and was stunned at the difference it immediately made in productivity. From this day on, I've been much more consistent in making the effort to hold regular prayer meetings with Him.

Thursday, January 9, 2014

William, be at peace. I love you. You're on the right track. Keep going. Progress is being made...more than you realize. ... You're not fighting me so this will work. You want to follow me and be obedient so you will be guided. The opportunity now is to relax and be open to receive and to take action in a smooth,

consistent manner. It is not requisite that you run faster than you have strength. But it is requisite that you run. You're pace is not my pace. Think of the moving walk ways at the airport. Sometimes you've run on those and sometimes you've walked. Sometimes you've rested or stood still and yet the movement forward continues. Get in My flow. My river is powerful and unstoppable. You've received important insights from Me regarding the flow of inspiration. Your joy in Me is wonderful and it will be wonderful even as you practice staying on the "moving" walk way when you see My hand rather than jumping off and reflecting on it enthusiastically. You can stay in the flow. I want you to stay in the flow so I can move you from one powerful moment seamlessly into another. ...meet with Me each day for 30 to 60 minutes. This will be the most productive time of your day. Everything that follows your time with Me will be more effective than the things you do in your day before meeting with Me.

This revelation is referenced in the section: Harness the Power of Forgiveness.

Friday, January 10, 2014

How can I let go of jealousy, envy, and covetousness?

All these come from a false sense of lack. Satan encourages you to focus on scarcity which is as core to his doctrines as abundance is to Mine. My abundance is everywhere regardless of what the world teaches. You've felt and experienced this and have therefore been able to be peaceful through what the world

69

would call poverty. Remembering your great riches in Christ both temporal and spiritual help you look outward to share and lift instead of being blinded and oblivious which causes you to look inward selfishly and fall for Satan's abusive tools you mentioned above—jealousy, envy, covetousness. Yes, he abuses you with these. This is why I command my children to put these tools of abuse down. Only when you hold them can Satan enter in and destroy. The ravages of Satan come through the portals of sin. These tools of abuse are so contrary to my ways that to hold or play with them in any degree puts you immediately in conflict or in opposition to me—which is sin—because they allow Satan to enter in and face me with you behind him where he hopes to imprison and enslave you permanently. Instead, I want you to trust in Me and pick up the tools of healing, strength, and power such as faith, forgiveness, love, hope, kindness and all the godly attributes because when you do, then you stand with Me in opposition to evil and I am able to keep you safe and progressing.

This revelation is referenced in the section: One-word answers or feelings or pictures are ok.

Sunday, March 30, 2014

First the spirit is born and is given an opportunity to grow and develop and mature.

Then the willing spirit experiences spiritual death or separation from Me as it leaves My presence and takes up residence in a tabernacle of clay—a physical body. ...

The physical body is subject to disease, temptation, and death. It has natural instincts to stay alive and to gratify passions, lusts, desires of the flesh. The flesh gives the spirit powers of sense it never had before, which powers of sense can bring a spectrum of new sensations from base, temporary happiness to lasting exultant joy. Because the body has no perspective but to experience sensation, it quickly succumbs to short term bursts of feeling. This inevitably leads to negative sensations and so begins a struggle to find happiness amidst a seeming never ending barrage of challenge, heartache, and problems of every sort.

The spirit has forgotten everything because of the veil and yet has senses of its own that feel after truth. Because the spirit senses truth it struggles to advise the flesh against careening out of control in the chase for feeling and pleasing sensation. When the spirit finds or is given guidelines and rules to follow (e.g. commandments), it usually wants to follow them and encourages the flesh to do likewise. Thus ensues the battle for mastery. The spirit is older, more mature, but must learn how to control the runaway flesh. This is done piece by piece through and with the power of the Gospel. Faith is the reign that pulls the flesh back into repentant subjection. Baptism is the formal acknowledgement that the natural man will no longer rule and reign. We symbolically bury the body and raise it up again into a new life where with the gift of the Holy Ghost, the spirit will take charge and be the master.

Master your body, William. Bring it into subjection. Let its voice be that of a humble servant willing to request water and food and rest but not demand it. Be a wise master, a loving master. Learn what your servant body needs to perform its optimal functions for you. See that it gets what it needs as it is respectful and obedient to you. When it seeks for pleasure and to pursue passions, see that those pleasures and passionate pursuits be anchored in building lasting treasures that endure beyond this earth, for where your treasure is, there will your heart be also. See that the pleasures and pursuits be tied to your wife, your children, the establishment of your eternal family and the building up of Zion. Deny the flesh all ungodly pursuits that would reward the flesh with temporary satisfaction in the doing of denigrating works. The pleasure habits of the flesh are difficult to change and so the placement of habits where pleasure in the body is felt must be governed with utmost care so that the power of the body be that of a servant... .

This revelation is referenced in the section: Choose to Believe.

Friday, July 11, 2014

Be at peace, My son. ... The constant pull of the fall toward death is no small thing. It's foggy and sloggy and difficult on a good day. Power, My power, is unchanging, anchored by faith to truth. It does not change with the weather, the times, or the advances in science and technology. The world is losing its anchor and increasingly moves with the tides and winds, very susceptible to deceit. You are building on the Rock. It takes time and consistency. The terminology of waxing often found in ancient records is like the growth of a tree, one ring at a time. Building on the Rock is a "waxing" process. It takes patience, especially when you can't see the results today. It can feel like things are passing you by as foundation-less buildings pop up seemingly overnight. The great and spacious building spoken of in the scriptures is a great example. This foundation-less structure was set in opposition to the Tree of Life—a tree! That which is built on the false doctrines of Lucifer will always diminish and fall. His doctrines are 100% about death and captivity regardless of the false advertising and deceiving varnish. My doctrines are 100% about life and the overcoming of death and hell by Christ, My beloved from the beginning. Worship of the false gods and idols espoused by Satan's doctrines bring a completely predictable result. They always lead to death and disappointment. When you worship Me, you are espousing the doctrines of life and setting your heart upon the things that endure and grow and live forever. To worship is to adore and to seek to become like. When you worship you imitate, and put your heart and soul into following. You make sacrifices to be where the focus of your worship is. You spend resources based upon the influence you allow from the god or God you follow. The stronger the worship, the more the attachment. The more the attachment, the more the influence. The more the influence, the greater the adoption of the associated doctrines and fruits of those doctrines.

The kindest commandment I've ever given My children is the first and great commandment: "Thou shalt love the Lord thy God with all thy heart, and with all thy soul, and with all thy

73

mind, and with all thy strength." See Mark 12:30, Deuteronomy 6:5 and 11:1, Matthew 22:37, D&C 59:5, Luke 10:27, etc... I know that if you are not giving your all to Me, then some of you is being misled toward a mischievous, destructive end. So I constantly invite and command that nothing in your life be placed ahead of Me. ... The more of you you give to Me, the more of your all you put into Me, the faster I can take you to perfect peace, happiness, and joy. Holding back from giving Me your all retards salvation. Yes, the fall has made claim on your soul. All of it. The atonement satisfied the claims of the fall, all of them. **Now, there is a dispute regarding who holds the deed to your soul. You are the judge that gets to resolve the dispute. That's called agency.** The lawyers, the agents of both sides of the argument are laying their cases before you. You get to decide how long the case will be reviewed before you. If you keep accepting the motions for more discovery, the appeals for re-trial, the objections for whatever rule or technicality that can be invented...then your decision gives breath to an on-going, perpetual court case. If you decide to personally try out the various actions brought before you rather than to make a decision at the bench; if you call a recess to personally experience every sort of idea laid before you...that's your decision. You are the judge. You have the power to decide and by eternal decree, no one can take that from you. Now, at the end of your term as judge, which coincides with your time on earth, you will be brought before the bar of a higher judge, the supreme judge, the highest judge of all judges even Christ himself. If your rulings have been just and align with righteousness and life then you will be given a reward of justness, righteousness, and life. If however, your rulings have been according to the doctrines of the fall; if you have decided in favor of Satan, then you will have as your reward the fruits of the fall. In other words, you get to live according to the power of the resurrection with the decisions, the rulings you made according to the court of your agency.

My case is laid before you to decide. I own you, William. I hold the deed to your soul and I ask you to decide in My favor. Here is the great and final evidence: I paid a terrible price to snatch you from the jaws of hell. I bled for you, I died for you. You were lost and fallen and now you're not. Choose Me and decide once and for all. Don't keep hearing the evidence from the opposing side. Don't keep entertaining their appeals. Cast them out from your courtroom. Let the gavel fall. Close the case. Step down from the bench. Join with Me. Take My yoke upon you. Let go, the heavy judges mantel. ...

This revelation was from a day I felt like I wasn't getting things right. I felt like a failure, like I was a disappointment to God. As is often the case when we let the world and its falseness get to us, the Lord sets things straight and gets us back on solid footing.

Thursday, August 28, 2014

William, My son, I understand everything you've said and all that is unsaid in your heart. I wish I might convince you with all the love I possess that you are not a disappointment to Me and that I am not disappointed by you. In fact, it's just the opposite. I'm pleased beyond what you can comprehend.

How Father, when I fall so short?

Because, William, My plan that you chose to follow was all about leaving My presence and going to a place of disarray where from the perspective seen by the eyes of the flesh it just isn't possible to succeed eternally for things there are in a state of constant decline. Without an infinite and eternal intervention, all would be lost forever and My plan for the eternal welfare of My children would have been frustrated.

But My plan has never been nor ever will be stopped or frustrated... .

...

The disappointment you feel when you think you have failed stems from false doctrines that feed the notion of separateness. Satan wants you to have no attachment to Me so that he can lead you down a path away from Me to hell. For this detachment to have a chance of working, he must convince you that:

a) you and only you are responsible for what you get in this life—this is the "man fairs according to his management of the creature" argument that can imply or assume there is no God and no devil and nothing after this life, or

b) you aren't measuring up to the requirements of your faith or religion so even if there were a salvation possible—which they argue is completely unreasonable—you don't qualify for it.

Both arguments really are the same argument: you must do it alone. The first argument says you must do it alone because there isn't any help "out there." The second argument says you must do it alone because, after all, you must "save yourself" by jumping through all the qualification hoops before your case can even be considered but since no such salvation exists it's all in vain anyway.

...

My grace is sufficient that all who come unto Me may be saved and as far as they desire to be saved.

...

Your sincere willingness to do My will is actually of greater importance to Me at this point than your ability to accomplish My will. As I have told you before, you are covered by the atonement. This is by covenant for you have—by your baptism and constant renewal in taking the sacrament—demonstrated your willingness to take upon you the name of My Son and your willingness to always remember Him and your willingness to keep His commandments. ... You are striving day by day to actually do what you are willing to do.

...

You are saved by grace, William, not by your works. Your works on the covenant path are all about becoming an active, willing participant in the journey. I freely let you into My home, onto the path without money or price. You cannot earn entrance to the path. Once entered in by the way, I invite you to come, follow Me. Learn of Me. Become like Me. Study, struggle, pray, practice, stumble, fall, do what you may but *be willing, remain willing, and let the willingness grow into a great desire as a seed growing into a tree of life until it becomes an active willingness. Then by the power of the Atonement, My grace is sufficient to change you into a new creature and take you all the way to Eternal Life.*

Do you see now why I'm not disappointed in you, William? Nor would I have you be disappointed. You are on the right path because you are on the path of growing, active willingness. Keep going and all will be well. ...

This revelation helped me learn one way Satan tries to get us to fear. The world without Christ would be dismal indeed; and that's the lie he tries to show us.

Friday, October 10, 2014

Keep breathing and trusting. Satan likes to point things out and paint a picture of things as they would be without Me in the picture. Don't fall for his unreasonable reasonableness. Hold things up in the light of Christ and truth across the broad spectrum of Eternity rather than a tiny unit of disconnected time separated from its context.

This revelation is referenced in the section: Don't be afraid to talk with God.

Wednesday, December 17, 2014

Fear not, William. I delight in the righteous desires of My children. When My children seek to become like Me, I rejoice. You cannot ask too much of Me as it regards this thing for indeed this is what I work for and desire. More often than not, it is the opposite that is of greatest concern—that My children ask nothing of Me or far less than what they could. ...

Your appetite for conversion has improved and you enjoy and welcome the changes. Repentance has become interesting and desirable to thee. The burdens of the world are giving way to the burdens of being a servant in My Kingdom. My burdens that I place upon thee are more like mantles of strengthening and enlargement to thy soul whereas the burdens of the world subtract and diminish the souls of man. Keep going, William.

This revelation is all about persistence and staying the course. As mentioned in the section *Keep wanting it!*, it's easy to get complacent or stop doing the things that help us progress. God doesn't want us to give up or think we can't take this journey. We can keep going and He will always help us!

Wednesday, June 10, 2015

William, be not disheartened because I have used more firmness with thee this morning. Your desires are good, your progress is wonderful. You don't want this progress to stop and neither do I. In order to continue your progress at the rate I know you can follow, there must be greater diligence and care to follow Me. Think of it like this: you want to go to places you've never been because you know that is the way to move to where I am. I say to thee, "follow Me," and you begin. I walk at a fast pace while assuring you that you can keep up if you will keep thy focus on Me and not look to the left or the right. And so we are walking quickly through a forest with dense underbrush. Ways are opening for Me because I know the path that no one else can see. I make it possible for you to walk through what seemed impossible barriers before. Things are going well and your confidence grows. Then your confidence turns to casualness which leads to sloppiness and you find that the passage through the forest slows a bit. You still see Me and are following but not at the rate you were and so a distance grows between us. Soon, the passage that was almost effortless before gets more cumbersome and then you find yourself seeing the barriers and the briers and your gaze is less on Me and more on what's blocking you. Finally, your march is nearly halted and it seems things are less possible and the rational mind tries to make sense of it, and then the excuses and self-justifications begin.

Now William, though this may happen a thousand times, I am willing to always come back for thee and start again. Please don't pretend this is not happening. By My atonement I've prepared a way for thee to always begin again and even pick up where you left off if you are willing to keep moving forward and not retreat back to former comfort zones. Let go of rationalizations and self-justifications. ... I know you perfectly.

I will go at a pace you can follow. It is not a pace of man or according to the ways of the world. It is a sustainable pace by My power and grace. Remember that and continually strive to attain the faith sufficient to stay the course.

Some final thoughts

Perhaps it goes without saying that I know God lives. Yet I'll never grow tired of saying it or sharing this basic, vital truth. Jesus Christ is the Son of God and Savior of mankind. I've been rescued so many times by Him I've lost count. He owns me because He's paid my debts and is now my "only" creditor. And by covenant, He has promised to own me before the Father at that great and last judgment day. His love is unfathomable. All I have and am or hope to be I owe to Him. My relationship with God and His Son means everything to me. I knew them before I came to earth, am getting re-acquainted with them now, and look forward to being with them again after my mission here on Earth is complete.

There are some choppy waters ahead and I'm not afraid. You don't need to be either. Christ's words have never been more needed: "In the world ye shall have tribulation: but be of good cheer; I have overcome the world." John 16:33

You have everything you need to take the next step with God, whatever that is for you. I hope you'll desire to move forward with Him. No one can take you further or faster than God can. My final words of encouragement are those I've heard repeated again and again in my mind over the

81

years through crazy up and down, hard and joyful times: "Trust in the Lord with all thine heart; and lean not unto thine own understanding. In all thy ways acknowledge him, and he shall direct thy paths." Psalms 3:5-6

May God, our loving Heavenly Father, bless us all In this journey of life. And may our desire to talk *with* Him deepen and increase a little more every day and our relationship with Him blossom eternally.

Made in the USA
San Bernardino, CA
12 April 2016